Children's History of the World

THE
ANCIENT
WORLD

OXFORD
Children's History of the World

THE
ANCIENT
WORLD

Neil Grant

OXFORD
UNIVERSITY PRESS

OXFORD
UNIVERSITY PRESS

Great Clarendon Street, Oxford OX2 6DP

Oxford University Press is a department of the University of Oxford.
It furthers the University's objective of excellence in research, scholarship,
and education by publishing worldwide in

Oxford New York

Athens Auckland Bangkok Bogotá Buenos Aires Kolkata
Cape Town Chennai Dar es Salaam Delhi Florence Hong Kong Istanbul
Karachi Kuala Lumpur Madrid Melbourne Mexico City Mumbai
Nairobi Paris São Paulo Shanghai Singapore Taipei Tokyo Toronto Warsaw

with associated companies in Berlin Ibadan

Oxford is a registered trade mark of Oxford University Press
in the UK and in certain other countries

First published 2001
Some material in this book was previously
published in Children's History of the World 2000

British Library Cataloguing in Publication Data available

Paperback ISBN 0-19-910822-6

1 3 5 7 9 10 8 6 4 2

Printed in Malaysia

CONSULTANTS
Mike Corbishley
Dr. Narayani Gupta
Dr. Rick Halpern
Dr. Douglas H. Johnson
Rosemary Kelly
James Mason

Contents

How to use this book

This book is divided into double-page spreads, each on a different subject. At the end of the book there is a Timeline. This shows at a glance the developments in different regions of the world during the period covered by the section. There is also a Who's Who page, which gives short biographies of the most important people of the period, a Glossary of important words, and an Index.

The text is divided into short blocks, each with its own heading. They describe one part of the main subject of the spread.

Dates here show the time in history when the events took place.

The title describes the subject of the spread, like a newspaper headline.

The first paragraph sets the scene, explaining what the spread is about and why it is important.

Early Cities

Settlements grew into towns and cities, where thousands of people lived, doing many different jobs. Some people became rich and powerful, but most were poor and forced to work very hard.

The growth of cities

The earliest cities in the world were built by people who had the most advanced farming, crafts and trade. Ordinary houses in the cities were made of cheap materials, such as mud bricks and thatch. Important buildings, like temples, were often built of stone. Remains of these buildings have been found, so we can imagine how they looked. The first region to develop cities was Sumer in southern Mesopotamia (modern Iraq). The cities were small states ruled by a king and nobles. The king also controlled all the settlements and farms in the region.

▷ The largest building in the Sumerian city of Ur was a ziggurat, a pyramid made up of huge platforms. On top was the temple where people believed Nana, the god of the city, lived. Because Sumer did not have much stone, even this building was made of mud bricks.

People start to write
People needed to write so that they could keep records. Early forms of writing used little pictures of objects. The Sumerians were the first to use symbols, like our letters. They wrote on clay tablets with a pointed tool. Because of the shape of the writing we call this cuneiform, which means wedge-shaped. This clay tablet records what crops were being grown in Sumer. Later, people began to write down religious stories.

Rulers and subjects

In the early city states there was a huge difference between the king, nobility and priests at the top of society, and the labourers and slaves at the bottom. In the middle were government officials, craftsmen and merchants. Although most people had to work from dawn until dusk, they had time off at religious festivals.

Ancient religion

The largest buildings in ancient cities were the temples. Religious beliefs developed from people's need to explain things they did not understand. For example, they realised that the Sun was important to life, so they believed the Sun was a god. Nana of Ur was a Moon god. Evidence from burial sites shows us that people believed in another life after death, and were buried with a religious ceremony.

Mathematics
The Sumerians were good at mathematics, probably because they needed to measure land. They invented a system of measuring in units of 60. The 60 minutes in an hour come from this system.

3500 BC - 500 BC

Arts in the early cities

Life in ancient cities was a struggle for many people, but richer people with leisure enjoyed music and art. They even played board games. Archaeologists have found many rich and beautiful objects at Ur made of gold, silver and stone. These show the great skill of the Sumerian jewellers and metalworkers.

◁ This ram or goat tied to a tree is made of gold, shell and lapis lazuli (a blue stone). It was made at Ur about 4,500 years ago, probably for a religious ceremony.

War between the cities

As far as we know, hunter-gatherers did not fight wars. Wars probably began when people first lived in large, permanent settlements. Sumerian cities were often at war with each other. The people built large, mud-brick walls to protect themselves.

◁ This scene shows the story of a king of Ur winning a battle. It starts on the bottom row with chariots charging at the enemy, and ends on the top row with the king inspecting his prisoners.

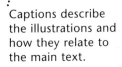

Captions describe the illustrations and how they relate to the main text.

Coloured boxes give more details about major events or important people linked to the subject.

Photographs and illustrations show paintings, objects, places, people and scenes from the past.

Fact boxes list key events associated with the subject.

Many pages also have a map, to show the country or region where the events took place.

Introduction

Historians learn about the past by studying all the written records they can find: government papers, books, personal letters, even things like tombstones or bus tickets. But as we go farther back in time, written records are fewer and fewer. For some ancient civilisations, there are none at all.

Luckily, we have other kinds of evidence. Archaeologists search for clues in objects that have been buried in the ground for hundreds or thousands of years. Not long ago, no one knew anything about the ancient civilisation of the Indus Valley, which existed in south Asia about 4,000 years ago. Now, thanks to archaeology, we know how the Indus people lived, what they ate, what kind of toys children played with.

This book, *The Ancient World*, begins with 'prehistory', meaning the time before history, when there are no documents for historians to study and few objects for archaeologists either. It covers the first civilisations in Africa and Asia, and ends after the fall of the Roman Empire, 1,500 years ago.

Two of the most important changes in history happened during this long period. The first was the invention of farming.

About 10,000 years ago human beings had to hunt for their food. Then they discovered how to grow their own crops from seed, and how to keep animals in flocks and herds. The very first farmers lived in the Middle East. Soon, groups of people in other parts of the world made the same discovery, although many hundreds of years passed before farming spread to all the parts of the world where it is possible. Farming meant that food could be produced more easily and in large amounts. As a result, the human population which had not changed much in thousands of years, grew much larger.

The second great change was a result of the first. Farming allowed people to settle down and live in one place. Villages grew, and human life became more complicated. The speed of change increased. In a few places, villages of mud huts grew into cities of stone. Civilisation had begun. People were no longer just hunters. Some were farmers, some were craftsmen, some rulers, and some slaves. Art, religion and education developed – and so did war. Writing was invented, and 'history' began.

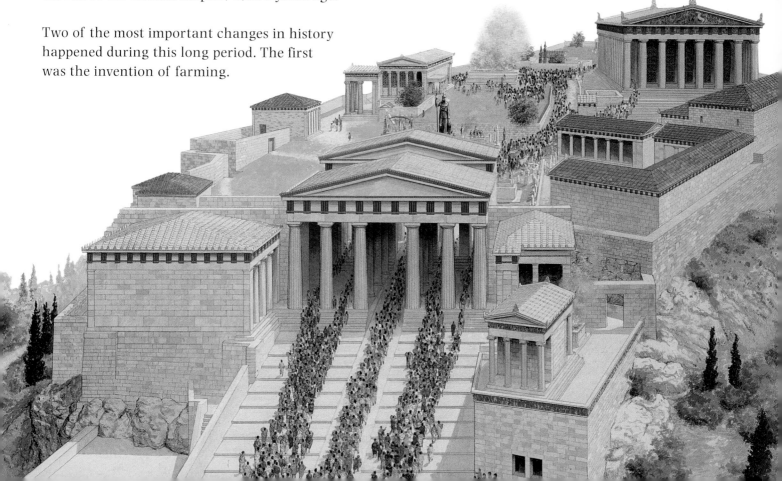

Early Human Beings

Our earliest ancestors first appeared on the Earth about 5,000,000 years ago. Modern humans, who looked like us, developed more recently, only about 40,000 years ago. They lived a simple life, hunting animals, and picking fruits and vegetables.

Humans spread across the world

Humans today do not all look alike. But we are all related. Everyone in the world today is probably descended from one small group of people.

Our earliest ancestors lived in east Africa. Their descendants spread to south and west Africa and, over many thousands of years, throughout the world. They walked across the narrow 'bridge' of land that divides the Mediterranean and the Red Sea from Africa, into Asia and Europe.

The Earth was much colder then, and the Arctic ice stretched south to where Paris and New York are today. Because so much water was frozen, sea levels were lower, and people crossed from Siberia to Alaska on foot. They moved slowly south through North, then South America. People from south-west Asia reached Australia by raft. Others set out by boat and settled on distant Pacific islands. Almost the last land to be settled was New Zealand, where the Maoris' ancestors arrived between 2,000 and 4,000 years ago.

▷ Beginning in Africa, humans spread across the world. The differences in appearance we see today are the result of chance and local conditions. All peoples are closely related. There is only one human race.

Our earliest ancestors

The scientific name for modern humans is Homo sapiens ('wise man'). Homo sapiens evolved from earlier humans, such as Homo erectus ('upright man'). The earlier humans were descended from human-like creatures called hominids. One of the earliest hominids was Australopithecus. Neanderthals were another form of Homo sapiens. They became extinct.

Australopithecus, early hominid

Homo erectus 'upright man'

Neanderthal man

Homo sapiens, modern man

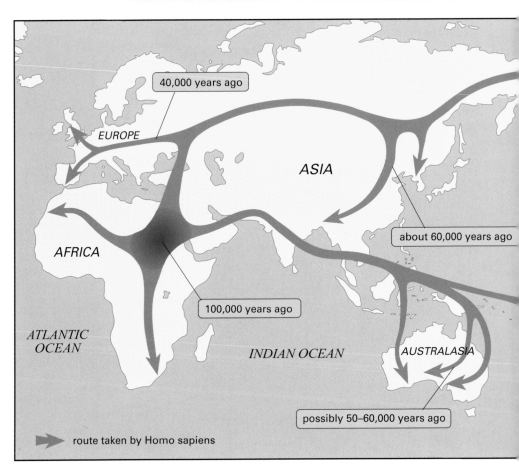

40,000 years ago

EUROPE

ASIA

AFRICA

about 60,000 years ago

100,000 years ago

ATLANTIC OCEAN

INDIAN OCEAN

AUSTRALASIA

possibly 50–60,000 years ago

➤ route taken by Homo sapiens

Hunters and gatherers

Early humans hunted animals and gathered wild plants for food. They also used the animal skins to make warm clothes. Their bigger brains, speech and agile hands gave humans an advantage over other animals. They lit fires and used tools. As they often moved in search of food, they made only simple shelters. We know that these people buried their dead carefully in graves, so they probably had some kind of religion. On the walls of caves they made wonderful paintings of animals. Perhaps these were a magic charm to give them luck in the hunt. As time passed, their skills increased, but human life changed little for 30,000 years.

▷ Neanderthal hunters in Europe trapped large animals, like this woolly rhinoceros, by digging big holes which they hid with branches.

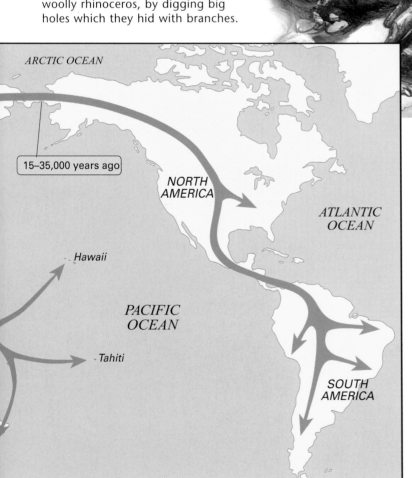

15–35,000 years ago

ARCTIC OCEAN

NORTH AMERICA

ATLANTIC OCEAN

Hawaii

PACIFIC OCEAN

Tahiti

SOUTH AMERICA

◁ Early humans made tools from wood, bone and stone. Flint was the most useful. It could be made into a hard chopper.

The end of the Ice Age

About 11,000 years ago the climate grew warmer. People moved further north, into lands uncovered when the ice melted. In these new lands they had to learn new habits and new crafts to survive. They made bows and arrows, fishing nets, and canoes from tree trunks. Life began to change more quickly.

The First Farmers

About 10,000 years ago the lives of some humans began to change. Instead of travelling in search of food, they settled down and learned how to grow food and keep animals. This gave them time to develop new skills, such as making pots, weaving cloth and using metals to make better tools.

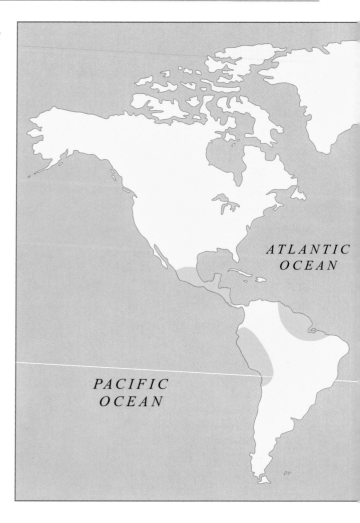

Early farm animals

Hunters often followed wandering herds of wild animals, which gave them meat for food and skins for clothes. As they gained control over these herds, the animals became partly tame. Europeans were riding horses and Africans were keeping cattle even before people began to grow crops. Many early animals looked different from the farm animals we have today. This early pig looks more like a wild boar.

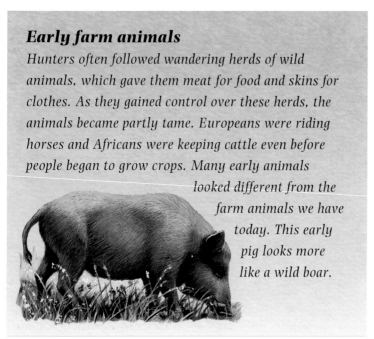

The first crops

Farming began about 10,000 years ago, after the end of the Ice Age. In some regions, people settled in one place, they collected the seeds of wild grasses, and learned to grow the ones which produced the largest grains. Different crops grew better in different parts of the world.

These first farmers lived in warm countries. They settled near big rivers because they needed a good supply of water. The very first farmers probably lived beside the Euphrates and Tigris Rivers in the Middle East, in a region called the Fertile Crescent. This region was much wetter than it is today, and crops grew well there. From there, farming spread very slowly to Europe and Africa. Meanwhile, people had begun farming in other parts of the world.

▽ The earliest pottery was made by hand. The potter's wheel was only invented thousands of years later. The first plough was just a pointed stick, which broke up the ground but did not turn the soil over.

The start of trade

As people began to make better use of the land, they produced more crops than they needed. This led to the growth of trade, as people exchanged the goods they had for the goods they needed. People living by the sea, for example, would have had plenty of fish but not enough wood for building. They could trade their fish for timber from a settlement further inland. Expert potters might trade with neighbours who made fine cloth.

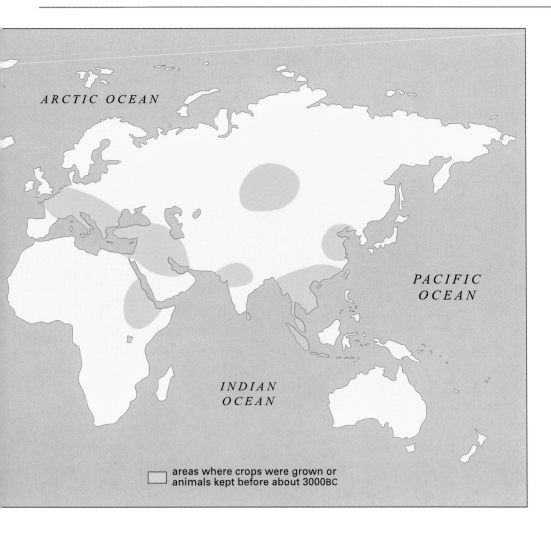

◁ The first farming regions. In the Fertile Crescent the main cereal crop was wheat. In the Far East it was millet, later rice, and in tropical America it was maize (sweet corn). In regions where it was too dry or the soil was not good for growing crops, people remained hunter-gatherers or herdsmen into modern times.

areas where crops were grown or animals kept before about 3000BC

Early crafts

When people became farmers they had a better food supply, so the population grew and began to settle in villages. Farming took less time than hunting and gathering food, which meant people had more time to develop crafts. The oldest crafts were making clothes, tools and pots. People made pots of baked clay 8,000 years ago. They also made woollen clothes, using wool from their sheep. The cloth was woven on a loom. People also made jewellery and ornaments.

▽ Different peoples learned to work in metal at different times. In China, it started much later than in the Near East. This Chinese bronze cooking pot was made in about 1700 BC.

Metalwork

Early farmers worked with wood or stone tools. Metal made better tools, but was hard to get. People found rocks with metal ore inside, and heated them to get the metal out. The ore melted and drained out. The first metal people learned to work with was copper, but this was too soft to make good tools. When they mixed it with tin, they made bronze, which was harder. Iron was best, but was more difficult to make. It came into use only about 4,000 years ago.

Early Cities

Settlements grew into towns and cities, where thousands of people lived, doing many different jobs. Some people became rich and powerful, but most were poor and forced to work very hard.

The growth of cities

The earliest cities in the world were built by people who had the most advanced farming, crafts and trade. Ordinary houses in the cities were made of cheap materials, such as mud bricks and thatch. Important buildings, like temples, were often built of stone. Remains of these buildings have been found, so we can imagine how they looked. The first region to develop cities was Sumer in southern Mesopotamia (modern Iraq). The cities were small states ruled by a king and nobles. The king also controlled all the settlements and farms in the region.

▷ The largest building in the Sumerian city of Ur was a ziggurat, a pyramid made up of huge platforms. On top was the temple where people believed Nana, the god of the city, lived. Because Sumer did not have much stone, even this building was made of mud bricks.

People start to write

People needed to write so that they could keep records. Early forms of writing used little pictures of objects. The Sumerians were the first to use symbols, like our letters. They wrote on clay tablets with a pointed tool. Because of the shape of the writing we call this cuneiform, which means wedge-shaped. This clay tablet records what crops were being grown in Sumer. Later, people began to write down religious stories.

Rulers and subjects

In the early city states there was a huge difference between the king, nobility and priests at the top of society, and the labourers and slaves at the bottom. In the middle were government officials, craftsmen and merchants. Although most people had to work from dawn until dusk, they had time off at religious festivals.

Ancient religion

The largest buildings in ancient cities were the temples. Religious beliefs developed from people's need to explain things they did not understand. For example, they realised that the Sun was important to life, so they believed the Sun was a god. Nana of Ur was a Moon god. Evidence from burial sites shows us that people believed in another life after death, and were buried with a religious ceremony.

Arts in the early cities

Life in ancient cities was a struggle for many people, but richer people with leisure enjoyed music and art. They even played board games. Archaeologists have found many rich and beautiful objects at Ur made of gold, silver and stone. These show the great skill of the Sumerian jewellers and metalworkers.

◁ This ram or goat tied to a tree is made of gold, shell and lapis lazuli (a blue stone). It was made at Ur about 4,500 years ago, probably for a religious ceremony.

War between the cities

As far as we know, hunter-gatherers did not fight wars. Wars probably began when people first lived in large, permanent settlements. Sumerian cities were often at war with each other. The people built large, mud-brick walls to protect themselves.

◁ This scene shows the story of a king of Ur winning a battle. It starts on the bottom row with chariots charging at the enemy, and ends on the top row with the king inspecting his prisoners.

Mathematics

The Sumerians were good at mathematics, probably because they needed to measure land. They invented a system of measuring in units of 60. The 60 minutes in an hour come from this system.

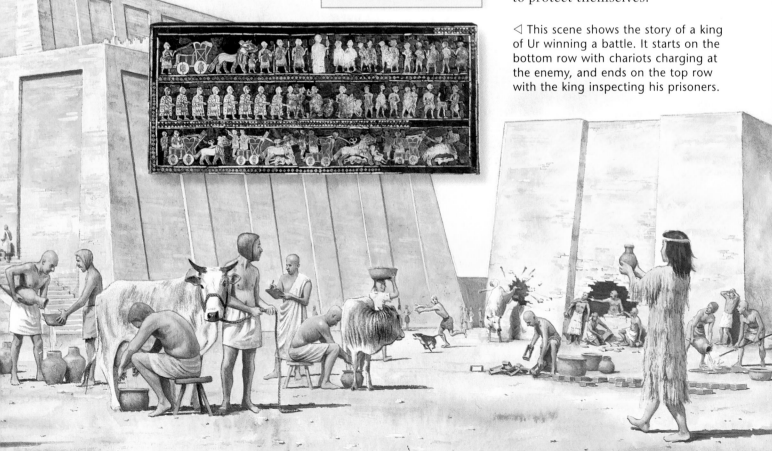

Ancient Egypt

The ancient Egyptians formed the first true nation 5,000 years ago. Their civilisation lasted for almost 3,000 years. The pyramids, built 4,500 years ago, are still standing at Giza. They remind us of the skills and wealth of Egypt's ancient civilisation.

▷ The River Nile flooded every year, creating a strip of rich farmland beside it. The surrounding deserts and sea kept Egypt safe from attack.

Mediterranean Sea

Nile Delta

LOWER EGYPT

Giza
Memphis

Nile

Tell el Amarna

Red Sea

UPPER EGYPT

Valley of the Kings — Karnak
Luxor

Aswan

Abu Simbel

Pharaoh and people

The king of Egypt, called the pharaoh, was all-powerful. In fact he was a god to the Egyptians, and had his own temple. Gods and temples were looked after by priests. The priests and officials (called scribes) also ran the government. Below them in society came the farmers, craftsmen and workmen, including slaves. Ordinary people had to work for the pharaoh, building huge palaces and temples, as well as working in the fields.

Although most people were poor, they had holidays and ate well. They could catch fish in the Nile, and hunt birds and animals in the Nile Delta. They also grew crops. The fields were fertilised with mud from the Nile. People used the Nile to water the plants. Farmers grew many different vegetables, grapes for wine, grain to make bread and beer, and flax to make linen clothes. They kept most of the types of animal found on farms today.

▽ The Nile was Egypt's heart and its highway. Here, people take water from the Nile. Boats carry people across the river. Men with nets fish from the riverbank and boats.

Royal riches

This coffin was made for the pharaoh Tutankhamun, who died aged 18 in about 1352BC. It is made of 110 kg of solid gold. The coffin was inside two larger wood coffins, decorated with gold-leaf. When Tutankhamun's tomb was found in 1922 it was full of beautiful treasures, including the throne he used when he became king at the age of nine. Tutankhamun was the only pharaoh whose tomb was not robbed in the centuries after his death.

Life after death

Most of what we know about the ancient Egyptians comes from their tombs. They believed in another life after death, where the dead would need their bodies. So the bodies of important people were preserved, in a complicated process called mummification. The mummy was buried in a stone tomb, along with things that the dead person might need in the afterlife, such as food and money. One pharaoh's tomb contained a model brewery, so he could drink beer in the next life.

Tombs also contained records of the dead person's life, in the form of pictures and writing. Egyptian writing used little pictures as symbols, called hieroglyphics. They also wrote on a form of paper, called papyrus, which they made from reeds.

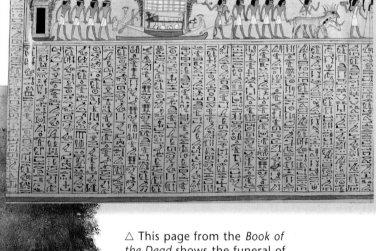

△ This page from the *Book of the Dead* shows the funeral of a man called Ani. Underneath is written a spell to help Ani in the afterlife.

3000 years of civilisation

3100BC	Egypt united by the pharaoh Menes.
2600-2160BC	The Old Kingdom. Pyramids built.
2160-2040BC	Central government breaks down.
2040-1700BC	Middle Kingdom. Egypt united again.
1700-1570BC	Egypt invaded by foreigners.
1570-1070BC	New Kingdom. Egypt at its greatest.
1070-600BC	Egypt broken into small states.
332BC	Egypt conquered by Alexander the Great.

Mesopotamia

For more than 2,000 years, empires rise and fell in Mesopotamia (modern Iraq). Many different peoples came to the region, some as conquerors, some as slaves. There were several empires at different times, but each one was affected by the ideas and customs of the Sumerians.

Babylon

The rulers of Babylon took control of many other cities in Mesopotamia. Their empire, Babylonia, was the greatest empire of ancient Mesopotamia. It ruled the whole region only for short periods, but it was never forgotten. It included the old cities of Sumer, and Babylonians inherited Sumerian inventions such as cuneiform writing and wheeled carts. Their arts and crafts were in the same style.

Babylon was built in about 1900 BC on the Euphrates River. It was a beautiful city, famous for its gardens and waterways. Canals were used for transport, and to take water out to the fields. Some were built on causeways, above ground level. Babylon was a rich and busy city, a great centre of trade. Money in the form of silver bars was borrowed and lent. Official records were kept of property and business, and wages were set at fixed rates. The temples of the gods of trade were used for business meetings. To control everything, King Hammurabi, Babylonia's most important ruler (1792-1750 BC), produced a system of laws. These were the first laws ever written down. They were also strict. Many crimes were punished by death.

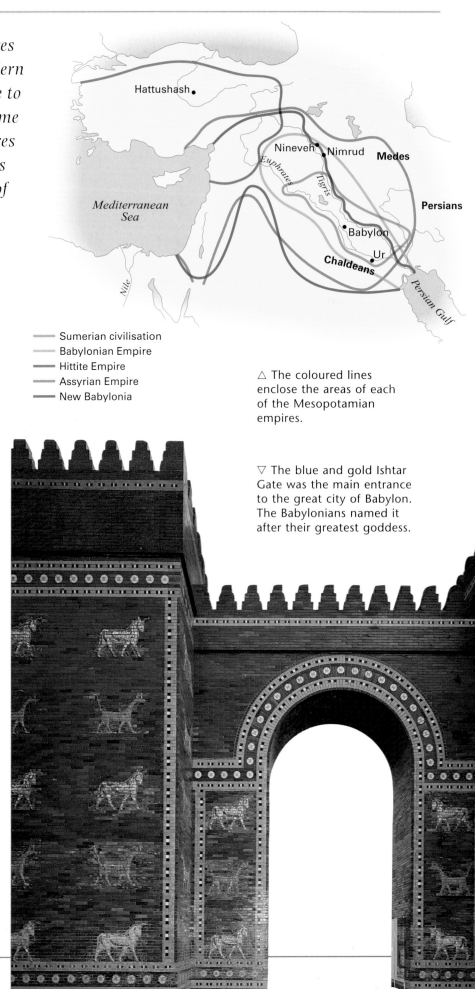

Map labels: Hattushash, Nineveh, Nimrud, Medes, Euphrates, Tigris, Persians, Mediterranean Sea, Babylon, Ur, Chaldeans, Nile, Persian Gulf

— Sumerian civilisation
— Babylonian Empire
— Hittite Empire
— Assyrian Empire
— New Babylonia

△ The coloured lines enclose the areas of each of the Mesopotamian empires.

▽ The blue and gold Ishtar Gate was the main entrance to the great city of Babylon. The Babylonians named it after their greatest goddess.

The Hittites

The Hittites came from southern Turkey. They were a warlike people, who used iron weapons, and they were the greatest power in Mesopotamia in about 1400-1200 BC. Although they destroyed Hammurabi's magnificent city, the Hittites were quick to copy Babylonian ideas. They had many skills, and some of them spoke eight languages. They had their own laws, which were less severe than Hammurabi's. But the Hittites were too ambitious. Their empire finally collapsed because they fought too many opponents at once.

Assyria

The black-bearded Assyrians were even more successful warriors than the Hittites. They conquered the Hittites in the 8th century BC, and took over their empire. Their well-trained soldiers were experts in chariot warfare. As they were quite a small nation, they also hired foreign soldiers to fight for them.

▷ The Assyrians were experts at using chariots in battle. They used the same skills when hunting. This carving shows King Ashurnasirpal II hunting lions. It once decorated his palace at Nimrud.

The Assyrians were not just gifted in warfare. Their cities were splendid. The walls of their mighty palaces were covered with sculptures showing the deeds of their kings. In the palace at Nineveh, archaeologists have discovered a large library of clay tablets. Among them was the world's oldest written story, the tale of the hero Gilgamesh.

New Babylonia

As Assyrian power faded, Babylon rose again, ruled by the Chaldeans, from the south. The Babylonian king, Nebuchadnezzar (605-562 BC), completely defeated the Assyrians in 608 BC. The new empire, New Babylonia, lasted for less than 100 years, but it was a brilliant time in Mesopotamian civilisation. The Chaldeans are especially remembered as skilled astronomers. They could tell when an eclipse of the moon would happen.

▷ A silver cup found in the Persian city of Ecbatana. Like other early artists, the Persian silversmiths and goldsmiths were especially good at representing animals.

The Persian empire

The Medes helped the Chaldeans fight the Assyrians. The Medes were one of the Iranian peoples from the east who had often swept into Mesopotamia. Another Iranian people were the Persians. In 547 BC the Persian king, Cyrus, united the Medes and Persians. With amazing speed, he created the largest empire that the world had ever seen. It included all the lands of earlier Mesopotamian empires, and stretched from the Mediterranean to modern Pakistan.

The powerful Persian Empire brought many benefits to its conquered peoples. The most important of these was peace, as the empire was not challenged for 200 years. Farmers could work in their fields without being attacked, merchants traded without fear. Although the Persians were savage in battle, their government was fair and tolerant.

Ancient China and India

Two early centres of civilisation developed in Asia. Like the civilisations in Mesopotamia and Egypt, they depended on the good farming land provided by great river valleys. The centre of the first Chinese civilisation was beside the Huang He. The other civilisation was in the valley of the Indus, in what is now Pakistan.

China

The first cities and states in the valley of the Huang He (Yellow River) were started by powerful families, or dynasties, by about 1600 BC. Very soon there were signs of the beliefs and customs that would continue in China for over 2,000 years. They had a strong belief in law, and a religious respect for their ancestors, whose spirits were supposed to influence the gods. Other early developments were chopsticks to eat with, the use of money, and a system of picture writing. They produced works of art in bronze, ivory and jade (a hard green stone).

Craftsmen were also making fine goods, such as pottery and silk, for which China would be famous 2,000 years later.

Life in the Huang He valley was not peaceful. There were wars between the small city-states, until the Qin dynasty finally united the Chinese people in 221-206 BC. The Qin ruler took the title of emperor, to show he ruled over the lesser kings.

The terracotta army

The first Qin emperor, Shihuangdi, was a harsh and powerful ruler who tried to take his power beyond the grave. Nearly 10,000 soldiers with their weapons and horses guarded his tomb near the Qin capital, Xi'an. But these were not real soldiers. They were life-size models made of baked clay (terracotta). In an amazing discovery, archaeologists found the emperor's tomb and his hidden army in 1974.

The Han dynasty

The Qin dynasty was followed by the Han dynasty (206 BC - AD 220). This was the first 'golden age' of imperial China. China became the most advanced country in the world, and the Han capital, Ch'ang-an, was the world's greatest city. Inventors discovered how to make porcelain and paper. Government officials had to pass examinations, and they ruled well and honestly. Han armies increased the size of the empire, and merchants traded outside its borders.

▽ The Great Wall of China is the largest building in the world. It is over 2,000 km long, 9 metres high and up to 5 metres wide. It was built to stop nomadic tribes in the north raiding China's rich cities and villages. The first Qin emperor strengthened it by joining the parts already built. Thousands of ordinary people were forced to work on it. Many died in accidents or from disease or overwork.

Confucius

Confucius was a great Chinese teacher, who lived about 500 BC. In later times, his teaching became a religion, but what he really taught was how to live in a civilised way. Confucianism was mostly about life on Earth. The Chinese believed in spirits and demons, but they had no all-powerful gods, no heaven or hell.

The Indus Valley

Of all the ancient civilisations, the one in the Indus Valley is the least well known. Although it lasted a thousand years, it was rediscovered only 150 years ago, by engineers building a railway. No one so far has been able to understand its written language. The mud-brick cities, which were built before 2000 BC, are still being studied by archaeologists.

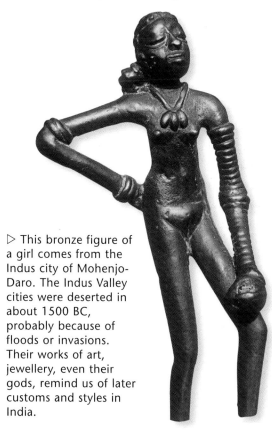

▷ This bronze figure of a girl comes from the Indus city of Mohenjo-Daro. The Indus Valley cities were deserted in about 1500 BC, probably because of floods or invasions. Their works of art, jewellery, even their gods, remind us of later customs and styles in India.

The people of the Indus Valley did not build huge temples or palaces. Their cities were carefully laid out, with roads and sewers. Some houses even had lavatories. Their largest buildings were storehouses for grain, which were huge so their harvests must have been good. They traded crops for copper, and they even had some contact with Mesopotamia. As well as food crops, they also grew cotton – they may have been the first people to do this.

The Mediterranean

*The first European civilisation developed on the island
of Crete in the middle of the Mediterranean Sea. It is
called the Minoan civilisation, after its legendary king
Minos. The Minoans were a sea-going people and grew
rich through trade.*

▽ This wall painting from the palace
at Knossos shows acrobats vaulting
over the back of a charging bull. This
custom was probably connected with
a religious ceremony. Bulls were the
most powerful animals known, and
they played a part in the beliefs of
many early peoples.

The Minoans of Crete

The Minoans lived on the fertile island
of Crete. They traded with Egypt, Greece
and Spain, and although they had no
army, their ships ruled the sea. Their
biggest city, Knossos, built before
2000 BC, had no city walls, which
shows that the Minoans had no fear of
invasion. Knossos had space for over
20,000 people, more than lived in
Babylon. It had paved roads, and the
water and sewage system was even
better than in the Indus cities. However,
the rich civilisation of the Minoans was
forgotten until archaeologists found its
remains less than 100 years ago.

We cannot read the Minoan language, so
we have to learn about the Minoans from
what archaeologists have found in Crete.
As well as jewellery and pottery, there
are lifelike wall paintings which
tell us a lot about Minoan
life. We know that the
Minoans were
ruled by kings,
who lived in big,
airy palaces.
The most
important
figure in
Minoan
religion was a
goddess. We do not know
her name, but she is often
pictured holding snakes, which
were a sign of long life and good health.

The Phoenicians

The Phoenicians were great seafarers from the coast of Lebanon. Until about 1200 BC they were ruled by powerful neighbours, such as Egypt. They never formed a single state, and their cities, including Sidon and Tyre, had their own rulers.

The Phoenicians were skilful craftsmen and traders. Although their country was small, it was fertile, producing grapes, olives and building timber. The tall cedars of Lebanon supplied timber to Mesopotamia and Egypt. The Phoenicians' most valuable export was a purple dye made from shellfish. They also traded goods from Africa and India. Like the Minoans, they set up colonies around the Mediterranean. The greatest was Carthage in north Africa, which became a great power in the Mediterranean after the Phoenicians' homeland was conquered by the Assyrians in the 7th century BC.

▷ Phoenician craftsmen made this perfume bottle by building it up in coils of molten glass. They may also have been the first to discover how to make glass vessels by blowing into a lump of molten glass on the end of a tube.

◁ The magnificent royal palace at Knossos was five floors high. It had thousands of rooms and covered an area as big as two soccer pitches. It was ruined by a huge volcanic explosion that destroyed the Minoan cities in about 1450 BC.

The first alphabet

The Phoenicians' greatest invention was their writing. They were the first to represent a sound with a single shape, which we would call a letter. This was the basis of our alphabet. Words were made up of several different shapes. This was different from Chinese writing where one shape represents a whole word.

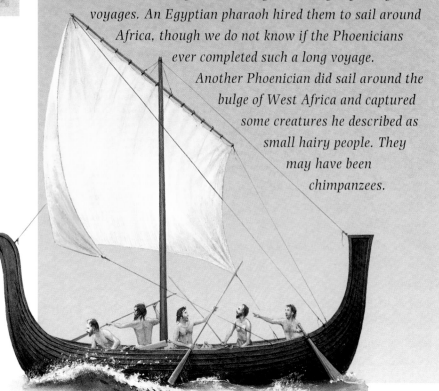

Voyages of trade and exploration

The Phoenicians developed tough little sailing ships, in which their sailors and merchants made long voyages. They sailed as far as Britain to buy tin, and they made long exploring voyages. An Egyptian pharaoh hired them to sail around Africa, though we do not know if the Phoenicians ever completed such a long voyage.

Another Phoenician did sail around the bulge of West Africa and captured some creatures he described as small hairy people. They may have been chimpanzees.

The Mycenaeans and Greeks

Mycenaeans from mainland Greece took over Crete in about 1450 BC. Their civilisation in Greece lasted nearly 300 years, before it was overcome by the invasion of a northern people, the ancestors of the ancient Greeks.

△ A gold mask (made after death) found in a Mycenaean grave by the archaeologist Heinrich Schliemann in 1876. Schliemann liked to think it portrayed the mythical Mycenaean king, Agamemnon.

Mycenae

The Mycenaeans were a stronger and more warlike people than the Minoans. They took over the Minoans' trade and colonies, and solid gold objects found in Mycenaean graves tell us they were very wealthy. They were less skilful craftsmen than the Minoans, and their cities were more strongly fortified. Each city had its own king. The kings were supported by landowning warriors, who ruled over the peasants and slaves. Although the cities were separate, in times of trouble they sometimes united. Mycenae, the city which gave its name to the whole people, was smaller than Knossos.

◁ The Aegean world, about 2000-1200 BC.

The Trojan war

Some historians think that the Mycenaeans went to war with the city of Troy in Asia Minor in the 12th century BC, probably over trade. This may have been the war described by the poet Homer, although he said it began when the Trojans kidnapped a princess. No one knew whether Troy really existed, until archaeologists discovered its remains in the late 19th century. There had been at least nine ancient cities on the site. When one was destroyed, another was built on the ruins. Remains of the different cities are found in layers, with the oldest at the bottom. Homer's Troy was probably the seventh city. Evidence shows that this was destroyed in about 1200 BC, just at the time that the siege in Homer's story took place.

The ancestors of the Greeks

Wars between their cities weakened the Mycenaeans, and so they were unable to stop invasions from the north. Among these invaders were a people known as Dorians, who were ancestors of the Greeks. Although their civilisation was less advanced, the invaders probably had better weapons made of iron. That gave them an advantage over the Mycenaeans, who used bronze. The Mycenaean cities were destroyed, and their treasures vanished. The art of writing was lost, and we know very little of what happened next in Greece, until the rise of Greek civilisation in about the 8th century BC.

▽ In Homer's story, the Greeks captured Troy by hiding some men in a huge wooden horse. They pretended to leave, and tricked the Trojans into hauling the horse inside the city walls.

Homer

The poet Homer, who lived in the 8th century BC, was the first great European writer. His two epics (long stories in verse), the Iliad and the Odyssey, tell the story of the siege of Troy and the adventures of the hero Odysseus (or Ulysses). The Greeks thought of Homer's heroes as their ancestors, but they were probably Mycenaeans. Although Homer was telling stories handed down over centuries, rather than history, we now know that Troy did exist and that there was a Trojan war.

The ancient Greeks

Some Mycenaeans fled from the invaders and settled in Ionia, on the west coast of Asia Minor (Turkey). Here they built strong cities, each ruled by a warrior king supported by nobles. On the Greek mainland, the invaders took over much of the south. Independent cities, with their own kings and gods, were also formed here and throughout Greece. Sometimes a ruthless leader, called a tyrant, seized power, and in many cities a struggle took place between rulers and people. By 500 BC, the ordinary citizens in a few city-states had some power. Athens, the largest city-state, was a true democracy.

People were proud of their own city, and neighbouring cities often made war on each other. But when, in the late 6th century, all of Greece was threatened by the growing Persian Empire, the rival cities, led by Athens and Sparta, joined forces and fought against the Persians. Their victory in this war united the Greeks and encouraged the development of the great civilisation of Classical Greece.

Classical Greece

The history of Western civilisation begins in Classical Greece in the 5th-4th centuries BC. The Greeks invented democracy, most kinds of literature, Western science, and even the Olympic Games. Greek ideas guided Europeans for 2,000 years.

The Greek city-states

The Greek city-states were communities, whose people had their own customs. These people thought of themselves as Greek, and they all spoke the same language, but their first loyalty was to their city. The city-states had different types of government. Sparta had a king and warrior nobles, while Athens was a democracy. Every male citizen who had been born in Athens voted and took part in government. Slaves and women could not vote, but women had some rights, and slaves could become free.

Greek art and architecture

The Greeks developed a wonderful style of architecture, and their sculptors made beautiful works in marble. Some of the buildings are still standing today. Greek pottery was decorated with paintings, often showing scenes from everyday life (below). These pictures are very useful to historians, because they show Greek customs, clothes, furniture, weapons and other objects.

▷ Crowds approach the entrance to the Acropolis, the religious centre of Athens. At top right is the Parthenon, the temple of Athena, patron goddess of the city.

Greek ideas

The Greeks owed many ideas to earlier civilisations. They especially admired Egypt, and they took the alphabet from the Phoenicians. But the Greeks went far beyond these earlier people. Athens produced some of the world's greatest thinkers. Much of their knowledge was new, and has influenced Europe ever since. In subjects like mathematics and biology, the Greeks were the greatest experts in Europe for more than 2,000 years. The ideas of philosophers such as Plato and Aristotle are still studied today. Although wonderful thinkers, the Greeks were not true scientists because they did not do experiments. Many of their ideas were wrong. For example, Aristotle thought that everything in nature is made up of earth, fire, air and water.

△ A marble bust of the philosopher Diogenes, who is said to have lived in a tub as a protest against people's bad behaviour.

Greek literature and theatre

The first true poets and historians were Greeks. That is one reason why we know so much about the Greeks. For the first time we can learn about people from their books. The theatre as we know it began with the great Athenian playwrights of the 5th-4th centuries BC. Aeschylus, Sophocles and Euripides wrote tragedies and comedies that are still performed today.

▽ Actors in Greek plays wore masks. These pottery figures are wearing masks for a comedy. Comic plays made rude jokes about politicians. Actors had different masks for acting in tragedies.

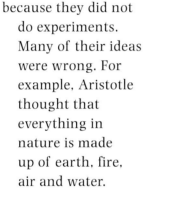

Greek gods

The Greeks had many gods and goddesses, led by Zeus and his family (Athena, goddess of Athens, was one of his daughters). Many were 'adopted' by the Greeks from eastern countries, and others were local gods. In stories the gods had supernatural powers, but also behaved like ordinary people. They quarrelled, told lies and lived everyday lives. To us, these gods are only legends, but most Greeks believed in them. Religious beliefs strongly affected life in Greece. Someone about to make an important decision would first ask a god for advice by going to a prophet, or oracle. There was a famous oracle at Delphi.

The Peloponnesian War

The rivalry between Athens and Sparta ended in a civil war. Every city in the Peloponnese (the southern part of Greece) took part on one side or the other. After nearly 30 years, Athens was defeated, and never recovered. The great days of the city-states were ending. Athens had given up democracy during the war. The Greeks were still not united, and although Persia was no longer a danger, there were others. King Philip of Macedonia, north of Greece, was planning to conquer the city-states.

Alexander the Great

Alexander of Macedonia was a great soldier and leader, who spread Greek influence over a large area. His empire stretched from Greece in the west to India in the east.

Macedonia's ambitions

The Macedonians were related to the Greeks and spoke Greek. However, the Greeks thought they were 'barbarians', which meant foreigners, and not true Greeks. The Macedonians were ruled by a king and a small class of warrior nobles, who trained the citizens into a good army. King Philip, Alexander's father, started taking over the Greek city-states one by one. He was murdered before his plans were complete, but his son Alexander made himself ruler of all the Greeks.

Alexander was the most famous warrior of ancient times. He carried out his father's plan to lead the Greeks against Persia, and launched his invasion in 334 BC, when he was 21. It was the beginning of a campaign that lasted until his death in 323 BC, when he was only 32.

▷ Alexander defeated the Persian king Darius at Issus (now in Turkey). By conquering the Persian empire, he had won most of the world that people in the Mediterranean knew. But Alexander wanted to conquer still more lands.

Alexander's empire

After defeating the Persian king in battle, Alexander marched through Syria into Egypt. There the people welcomed him and called him a god. He defeated the Persians a second time, and their whole empire collapsed. The king was killed by his own men, and Alexander replaced him as ruler.

This did not satisfy Alexander. Like all conquerors, he found it difficult to stop, but he was also driven by a desire to learn about the whole world. He marched on across Afghanistan and into north-west India, defeating an Indian prince whose army contained 200 trained elephants. At last, his tired men, who had been fighting for eight years, refused to go further. Alexander agreed to return home, but first he persuaded his men to march down the Indus valley to the ocean, which the Greeks believed circled the Earth. From there he led the long march homewards, but he died in Babylon before he reached Greece.

△ Alexander's conquests depended on good organisation. Although he travelled very far, he was always in touch with Macedonia.

→ route taken by Alexander the Great

The Greek world

Alexander's empire did not last long after his death. The Mauryan kings of eastern India reconquered the Indian lands, and the rest of Alexander's empire was divided among his generals. They founded ruling families in Egypt and the Middle East. Three centuries later, the remains of Alexander's empire became part of the Roman Empire.

Alexander tried to unite the East (the world of the Mesopotamian empires) and the West (Greece and the Mediterranean region). His empire depended on the support of the people of the conquered lands. To win them over he accepted some of their customs himself. He married a Persian princess, and forced thousands of his soldiers to marry Asian women. But he also spread the influence of Greek civilisation. The people in the cities he built followed Greek customs and spoke Greek.

△ After his death Alexander became a legend. One eastern king even had Alexander's victory at Issus carved on the sarcophagus he was buried in. A thousand years after the death of Alexander, stories about him were eagerly read, although they were mostly untrue.

Alexandria
Many cities were founded by Alexander, and named after him. The most famous is Alexandria in Egypt, which became a great centre of learning. Euclid, the founder of geometry, and Archimedes (above), who invented the screw, studied at the city's library. Eratosthenes, who was the chief librarian about 200 BC, measured the size of the Earth.

The Roman Republic

The ideas and customs of Classical Greece passed to the next great Mediterranean power, Rome. Starting as a small city state, over 500 years the Roman Republic won an empire as large as that of Alexander the Great.

The Etruscans

The Etruscans, whose ancestors had come from the East, ruled north-west Italy. In this very fertile land, their kings and nobles grew rich. One city ruled by the Etruscans was Rome. In about 509 BC the Romans rebelled, and threw out the Etruscans. For the next 200 years the Romans were usually at war. They won towns from the Etruscans, and defeated neighbouring peoples, until they became the largest power in Italy.

△ In 218 BC Hannibal, a great Carthaginian general, surprised the Romans by invading from the north. He led his army, including some elephants, across rivers and the Alps.

The Romans could not beat him in battle, but Hannibal could not capture Rome. After 15 years, he was called home to defend Carthage from Roman attack.

The Republic

The Romans did not want another king. They formed a republic, led by two officials called consuls, who were elected every year. The Plebeians, the ordinary people, could vote, but the chief noble families, the Patricians, had the real power. Their representatives made up the powerful Senate, or governing council. The Romans had a strong sense of duty to their family, and also to their state. This made them patriotic and determined warriors. After conquering Italy, they defeated the North African city of Carthage and gained control of the Mediterranean.

▽ The Romans built public baths in every city. Although they liked to keep clean, they also believed in games and fitness. The baths were a kind of sports and social club, where friends or business partners would meet.

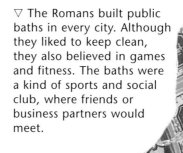

Roman religion

The Romans took much of their religion from the Greeks. The Roman god Jupiter is the same as the Greek god Zeus. As well as gods of the state, they worshipped family gods, who looked after the household or the farm.

Rich against poor

Fighting wars helped to keep Romans united, but trouble grew between the rich and powerful Patricians and the poor citizens, the Plebeians. The Plebeians won some victories. They were allowed to elect their own representatives, called tribunes, who formed their own assembly. But in the 2nd century BC the struggle between the classes brought Rome close to chaos. Government broke down, and many people on both sides were murdered. Civil war broke out in the next century between rival generals Marius and Sulla. Sulla won. He was a brutal ruler and no one was able to control him. He ruined the Republic.

◁ The Romans enjoyed cruel sports. Gladiators fought duels to the death, to entertain the Roman people. Sometimes they fought wild animals (left). Gladiators were often slaves or prisoners. There were a huge number of slaves in ancient Rome. At one slave sale, 150,000 people were sold in a day. A rebellion of slaves in 73 BC was crushed with great cruelty, after they had rampaged through southern Italy.

The end of the Republic

By the 1st century BC the Roman army had become the most powerful force in the Republic. It helped give Rome its first emperor. Soldiers in distant places were loyal to their own generals, not to Rome. After Sulla died, other generals struggled for power. The winning general was Julius Caesar, who had conquered Gaul (France) and invaded Britain. He defeated his chief rival, Pompey, and took power. Caesar's rule lasted only five years. He was murdered by a group of jealous senators, who were afraid that he was going to make himself a king. The murder caused another civil war, which was won by Caesar's friend Mark Antony and his nephew, Octavian. The winners then quarrelled. Octavian defeated Antony and became Rome's first emperor, known as Augustus.

▽ Cleopatra, the last queen of Egypt, used her beauty as a weapon in politics. She fell in love with Julius Caesar and they had a son. Later, she fell in love with Mark Antony. The defeat of Antony by Octavian in 31 BC ended Egypt's independence, and Cleopatra killed herself.

The Roman Empire

For 600 years the Romans ruled most of Europe, North Africa, and part of the Middle East. Roman law, ideas and customs influenced European civilisation for more than a thousand years after the Roman Empire had ended.

Roman rule

When they built their empire, the Romans killed many people and destroyed the customs and beliefs of many more. But most people of the conquered lands welcomed Roman rule and their more advanced standard of living. People in lands as far apart as Britain and Palestine were proud to be Roman citizens. Under Roman rule, people enjoyed fair government and peace. Two things especially held the empire together. One was Latin, the Roman language, which was spoken by educated Europeans for centuries. The other was Roman law, which was simple to understand and enforced fairly. In countries such as France, Roman law is still the basis of the legal system. Taxes were not too heavy, and the protection and good government of Rome allowed trade and farming to prosper. However, even the best Roman governors used their power to make themselves rich.

The emperors

Because Roman emperors had enormous power, much depended on their character. Some were fair and intelligent men like Augustus, the first emperor (above). Others were selfish and half-crazy like Nero, the fifth emperor, who was said to have set Rome on fire out of spite. The emperor was supposed to be elected, but in fact he was either the heir of the previous emperor or, in later times, the winner of a struggle between rival generals.

▽ A grand procession through Rome of the treasure taken during the capture of Jerusalem in AD 70.

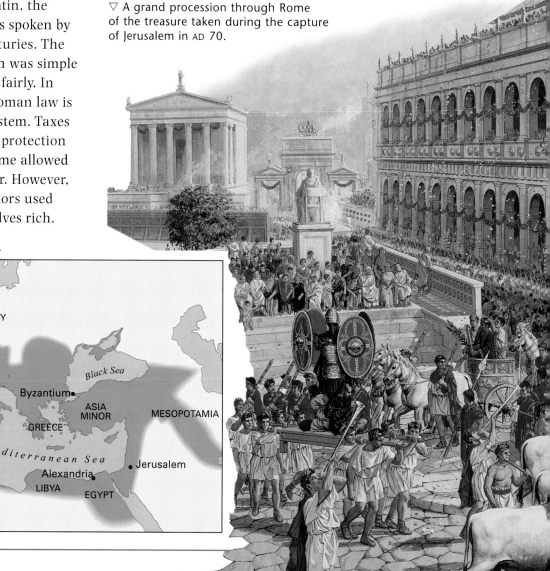

▽ The Roman Empire in AD 117.

BRITAIN
ATLANTIC OCEAN
GERMANY
GAUL
ITALY
SPAIN
Rome•
Pompeii•
Byzantium•
Black Sea
ASIA MINOR
GREECE
MESOPOTAMIA
Carthage•
Mediterranean Sea
AFRICA
LIBYA
Alexandria•
EGYPT
•Jerusalem

— Hadrian's Wall

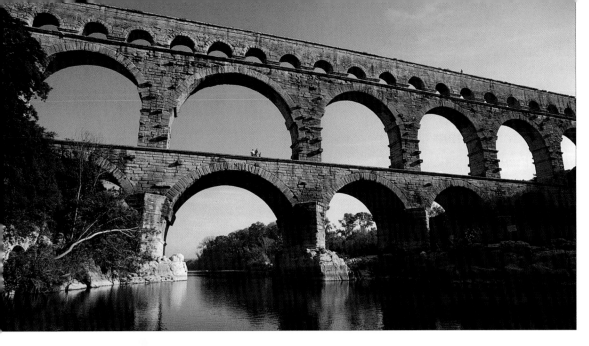

◁ The Pont du Gard, the great aqueduct over the valley of the River Gard in southern France, was built 2,000 years ago to carry fresh water to the Roman city of Nîmes.

Arts and technology

Roman civilisation owed a lot to the Greeks, but Rome had its own great writers, such as Virgil, Horace and Ovid. Romans were highly skilled, not only at organising an empire, but also in building and engineering. They thought their empire would last forever, and wanted their buildings to last as long. Many of them have lasted to the present day. Roman buildings had arches and domes, and were built with brick and concrete as well as stone. Palaces and rich men's villas had underfloor heating, which was useful in colder provinces such as Britain. The Romans also excelled in some crafts, particularly glass and mosaics.

The beginning of the end

The empire continued to expand until the time of Hadrian (AD 117-138), who decided it was already too big. He used the army for jobs like road building instead of conquest. From the 3rd century, 'barbarian' peoples from the north-east began to settle inside the empire. The imperial government had grown weak, Rome was no longer prosperous and, like all empires, the Roman Empire was running out of energy. It was later divided in two: a Western Empire ruled from Rome, and an Eastern Empire ruled from Constantinople (Byzantium).

The 'Barbarians'

In the 5th century, whole peoples from eastern Europe began to move west. The Huns, who came from furthest east, were the first to start moving. In the end, these 'barbarian' invasions destroyed both the Roman Empire in Europe and the Gupta Empire in India.

The Goths

The Goths were a farming people living by the Black Sea when the Huns invaded the region. They were allowed to enter the Roman Empire, but soon fell out with the Romans. In AD 378 they defeated the Romans in battle at Adrianople and killed the emperor Valens. They invaded Italy, but a Vandal general held them back for a while. The Romans could no longer defend themselves, and the Goths captured Rome in AD 410. The Goths were not just a fighting people. They also made beautiful objects like this silver buckle.

▷ The Huns, Visigoths, Ostrogoths and Vandals spread across Europe. The Huns also invaded Persia and India, and pushed European tribes further west. The Angles and Saxons settled in Britain.

The Barbarians and the Romans

The Romans, like the Greeks, called all foreigners 'barbarians'. The Germanic peoples who invaded the empire lived a simple life, but they were not savages. Some had been in contact with Rome for many years. They knew Roman customs and they admired the Empire, especially its wealth. They would have liked to take it over, but they were too disorganised to manage an empire. In the end they helped to destroy it. The movement of peoples from east to west was not new. The Celts in France and Britain had originally come from central Europe.

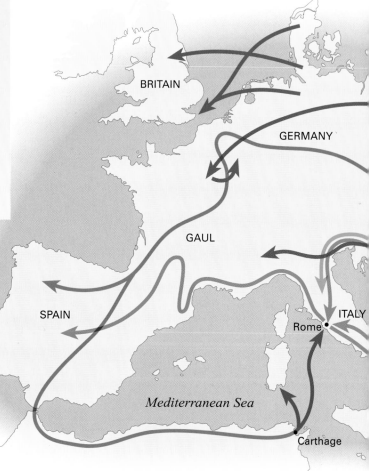

Huns
Visigoths
Ostrogoths
Vandals and Alans
Angles, Saxons and Jutes

BRITAIN

GERMANY

GAUL

SPAIN

ITALY
Rome

Mediterranean Sea

Carthage

The Huns

The Huns were a group of wandering tribes, who kept cattle but grew no crops. They also lived by hunting and gathering and, sometimes, by raiding settlements. They were brilliant horsemen, and their children learned to ride as soon as they could walk. The 'Black' Huns were the first people to move west in the 5th century, when they spread into eastern Europe, pushing other tribes, such as the Alans and Goths, further west. Another group, the 'White' Huns, turned south and invaded Persia, where they killed the emperor. They moved on into India, where they destroyed Gupta civilisation and set up their own kings. The Huns killed tens of thousands of people, and were renowned for their cruelty.

◁ A Hun horseman. Some people believed that Hun and horse were parts of one animal! The Huns used a short but deadly bow, easy to shoot from a horse. It was made from strips of wood, bone and sinew which had to be glued together when the weather was not too warm or too cold.

The end of Roman Empire

The Vandals, who came from north Germany, invaded Gaul in the early 4th century. They were driven south into Spain by the Visigoths (western Goths), and finally settled in Roman North Africa. They made Carthage their capital, and controlled the Mediterranean. In AD 455 the Vandals sailed across to Italy, captured Rome and took all the treasure they could carry.

Meanwhile, the Huns launched their greatest attack under their leader, Attila. In AD 447 they besieged Constantinople, capital of the East Roman or Byzantine Empire, but they agreed to leave the city for three tons of gold. They conquered much of the Empire and invaded Italy, but disease and hunger forced them out before they could capture Rome. However, they caused enough destruction to finish off the Roman Empire. The last emperor was deposed in AD 476 by Odoacer, a 'Barbarian' general who had at one time fought on Rome's side.

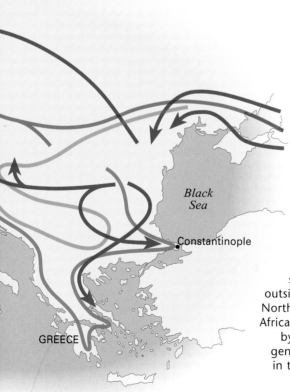

Black Sea

Constantinople

GREECE

▷ This mosaic shows a Vandal outside Carthage in North Africa. Vandal Africa was destroyed by the Byzantine general, Belisarius, in the 6th century

The Byzantine Empire

The Roman Empire in Europe collapsed in the 5th century AD. The Roman Empire in the East, called the Byzantine Empire, survived for a thousand years. It developed into a civilisation that was quite different from Europe.

▷ In Constantinople, Justinian built the Church of St Sophia, the largest and most beautiful Christian church of that time. When the Ottomans captured Constantinople in 1453, they turned St Sophia into a mosque.

Byzantium

The Roman emperor Constantine decided to make Byzantium his eastern capital in AD 330, and he changed the city's name to Constantinople (now Istanbul). It controlled trade routes between Europe and Asia and, while Rome was getting weaker, it grew into the largest and richest city in Europe. Its massive city walls are still an impressive sight.

The Byzantine emperors still called themselves 'Romans', and dreamed of reconquering Rome's Western Empire. After Odoacer defeated the last emperor of Rome, the Byzantine emperor, Zeno, paid the Ostrogoths to overthrow him. They succeeded, but to Zeno's annoyance, the Ostrogoth leader made himself ruler, and built a fine capital at Ravenna, in north-east Italy.

Orthodox Christianity

Constantine had made Christianity the religion of the Roman Empire, and so Byzantium was a Christian state. Religion was a part of government and of everyday life. The emperor was God's representative. In pictures he was shown with a halo, like a saint. In Europe the Pope led the Roman Catholic Church, but the Church in Byzantium had no religious leader. It used the Greek language, not Latin, and had different ceremonies. Growing arguments about religious customs drove the Roman and Byzantine Churches further apart. In AD 1054 they became completely separate. Byzantium also had its own style of religious art. Its most famous art works are icons (religious images) like this one of the Archangel Michael.

Justinian the Great

Under the Emperor Justinian, called 'the Great' (AD 527-65), the dream of restoring the old Roman Empire almost came true. Belisarius and other Byzantine generals reconquered North Africa, most of Italy and part of Spain. However, the Byzantines spoke Greek instead of Latin, and the Europeans thought they were foreigners, not 'Romans'. The Byzantines soon lost the reconquered lands, and Byzantium steadily lost contact with Europe.

Justinian ruled with his strong and intelligent wife, Theodora. He was the most successful Byzantine emperor, but he was less successful as a ruler after his wife's death. To us, his greatest achievement was not his brief conquests, nor even St Sophia, but his code of law. This preserved the laws which the Romans had made, for the future benefit of Europe.

The empire under siege

The Byzantine Empire was never as strong as it had been under Justinian. In spite of wonderful achievements in art and learning, the Byzantines were not good governors. They did not look after the peasants, who provided their food and fought in their armies. The emperors had many enemies abroad. In the 7th century the empire seemed about to collapse, but it was saved by a great general and emperor, Heraclius, who defeated the Slavs and Persians. But before his death a new, more powerful enemy appeared – the armies of Islam.

△ Byzantine artists were particularly famous for their mosaics. This one shows the Empress Theodora, wife of Justinian, with her attendants and officials.

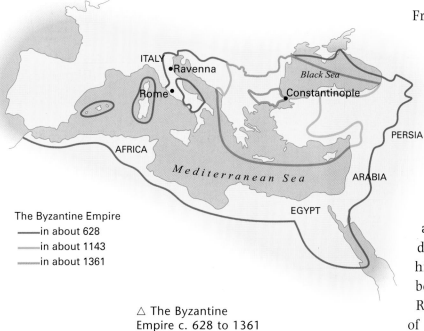

The Byzantine Empire
—— in about 628
—— in about 1143
—— in about 1361

△ The Byzantine
Empire c. 628 to 1361

From the 11th century, Constantinople was failing and its empire shrinking. The Byzantines were still fine artists and scholars. They kept alive ancient learning that Europe had forgotten. But, like ancient Rome a thousand years before, the Byzantines could no longer defend themselves. They had to hire foreign soldiers to help them. The Byzantine Empire finally ended when the Ottoman Turks captured Constantinople after a great siege in 1453. The last emperor died fighting, and a fine civilisation died with him. After the fall of Constantinople, Russia became the leading Orthodox country. The Russian tsars saw themselves as the heirs of the Byzantine emperors.

Religion

In history, religion has been one of the strongest influences on the way people think and behave. Most of the world's great religions began 2,000 years ago or more. Only Islam is more recent. All of these religions began in either India or the Middle East.

Hinduism

The oldest of current religions is Hinduism, which developed in India more than 4,000 years ago and spread to south-east Asia. Unlike most other religions, it had no founder or prophet, and no elaborate organisation. Its holy writings, the *Mahabharata* and *Ramayana*, were written more than 1,500 years ago. Hinduism has many different customs and beliefs, and hundreds of different gods. The main teaching of Hinduism is that people should do their work well and honestly, and live a morally good life. In ancient times Hinduism existed in India along with Buddhism and, later, with Islam. There were conflicts between the religions, but people mostly lived together peacefully.

△ The Hindu god Shiva dances in a circle of fire. Shiva the Destroyer is one of the three aspects of God. The others are Brahma (the Creator) and Vishnu (the Preserver).

▽ The Great Stupa at Sanchi, India, was begun by the Emperor Asoka, who helped to spread Buddhism. Stupas were Buddhist temples and contained relics.

Buddhism

Buddhism was founded by Siddhartha Gautama, called the Buddha, a prince who lived in north India about 2,500 years ago. The suffering of ordinary people inspired him to give up his princely life. He spent the rest of his days meditating and teaching. Buddha taught that all living creatures are reborn in another form, so all living things should be respected. The cycle of dying and being reborn ends when a person reaches a state of 'enlightenment'. This means he has overcome all selfish desires. Buddhism developed many different branches. It was eventually absorbed into Hinduism in India, but its teachings spread all over central and eastern Asia, including China and Japan.

Judaism

The Israelites, later called Jews, were a small group of people in Palestine whose religion developed more than 3,000 years ago. The most important idea in Judaism is the belief in a single, all-powerful God, who created the world and everything in it. Prophets, such as Abraham and Moses, told the people about God's instructions. The prophets were the real leaders of the Jews who, for most of their history, were ruled by greater powers such as Babylon and Rome. After Jewish rebellions in the 2nd century AD, most Jews were driven from Palestine and scattered across Europe and the Middle East. They kept their religion during the centuries of exile, but did not regain their homeland until the creation of Israel in 1948.

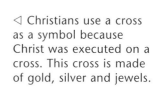

◁ Christians use a cross as a symbol because Christ was executed on a cross. This cross is made of gold, silver and jewels.

Christianity

Christianity developed as an offshoot of Judaism, following the teachings of a man called Jesus. Jesus Christ was born in about 4 BC ('Christ' means Saviour). His followers believed he was the Son of God. He stood up for the poor and he attacked the Jewish religious authorities. He promised a future kingdom of God, where the poor and humble would be rewarded. His powerful teaching worried the Jewish religious authorities and the Roman rulers, and he was executed in about AD 29. Christians believe that he came back to life and was taken to Heaven. They expect him to return one day to rule over the kingdom of God on Earth. More and more people became Christians, even though they were persecuted in the Roman Empire. However, in AD 313 the Emperor Constantine made Christianity the official religion of the empire. In the next few centuries, Christianity spread all over Europe, governed by a powerful organisation headed by the Pope in Rome.

▽ The prophets taught the Israelites to obey God. In one Bible story, when the Israelites began to worship a foreign god, Baal, the prophet Elijah challenged the priests of Baal, to see if God or Baal could set an altar on fire.

The Ten Commandments

The Ten Commandments were ten rules for living, written in stone. They were said to have been given by God to Moses on the top of Mount Sinai, while the Jews were making their long journey back from exile in Egypt to their homeland in Palestine, in about 1300 BC. The history of the Jews is written in the Old Testament, which also forms part of the Christian Bible.

The Americas

In the Americas civilisation developed later than in Asia and Europe. Different peoples and empires rose and fell in Central America over the centuries, but some traditions were passed on from one people to the next.

American civilisations

The first large cities were built more than 2,000 years ago. They were ruled by powerful kings, supported by warrior-nobles and priests. They appeared in two regions, in Central America and in South America west of the Andes Mountains.

The Olmecs were one of the earliest peoples in Mexico. They grew maize as their main crop, and were skilful sculptors, especially in jade. Their greatest centre, La Venta, was at its most important 900-400 BC. Most of its large buildings were temples, built on earth platforms. Later peoples continued that tradition.

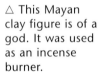

△ This Mayan clay figure is of a god. It was used as an incense burner.

The Golden Age of the Maya

The 6th century AD was a time of wars, and many different peoples established powerful centres in the Americas. The greatest were the Maya, in southern Mexico and Guatemala. Mayan civilisation took its traditions from the Olmecs. It was at its height about AD 300-1000, but it had not completely disappeared when the Spanish arrived in 1520. Mayan cities were centres of religion, and priests controlled much of everyday life. Their huge stone temples in the form of ziggurats were 60 metres high. The cities were independent powers, but were joined by good roads. Most of the people lived in villages, growing crops in fields that they cleared in the forest. The Maya were experts in some subjects, such as astronomy and mathematics. They had an accurate calendar and a written language. But they had no metal tools, and they never used the wheel.

◁ The Olmecs are known for their carving. This axe was made out of jade, for use in religious ceremonies.

The Aztecs

By the 15th century there were two great civilisations in the Americas, the Aztecs in Mexico and Incas in Peru. These were true empires, including different groups of people with different languages. The Aztec capital, Tenochtitlán, was a beautiful place with gardens, towers and canals. It was built on an island in a lake and reached by causeways from the shore. Over 500,000 people lived there. Other people of the Aztec empire lived in farming villages. They produced good crops of maize, although they had no ploughs, carts or animals to pull them. The bloodthirsty Aztec gods needed human victims, so the Aztecs fought many wars to capture prisoners for sacrifice.

▽ Tenochtitlán, the Aztec capital, had large ziggurats which dominated the city like the ones built in ancient Mesopotamia. At the top of the largest ziggurat (on the left) was a pair of temples. One was to the rain god, Tlaloc, the other was to Huitzilopochtli, god of sun and war. The remains of the city are now under the modern Mexico City.

The peoples of North America

The natives of North America lived in thousands of different groups, who spoke hundreds of different languages. The people of the Great Plains in the west were hunters, who lived off the buffalo herds and lived in tepees (tents). In other places, people farmed and lived in permanent villages. Some Pacific-coast people built wooden houses decorated with carvings and paintings, while the Pueblo people of the south-west made houses of adobe (mud bricks). Most peoples were ruled by kings and priests, who were usually the cleverest men of the tribe. They had many gods and spirits of nature, and celebrated festivals with singing and dancing.

The Incas

The Incas controlled most of South America west of the Andes. Their empire included about 8 million people. The chief cities were built high in the Andes mountains, and were connected by paved roads. Relay runners kept the rulers in touch with local affairs. All property belonged to the state, and was shared out among the people. Private life was governed by strict rules. Two people could not marry without government approval. Under Inca law, a blind man had to marry a blind woman. Special help was given to the old and sick, but this was not a 'welfare state'. The rulers, not the people, came first.

The Ancient World

For most of this period, we have no written records. Even after the invention of writing, the records are few and not always reliable. Most of our knowledge depends on the work of archaeologists, who have discovered such things as the remains of ancient cities.

	BEFORE 4000 BC	**4000–3000 BC**	**3000–2000 BC**	**2000–1000 BC**
AMERICAS	**c.14,000** People reach Alaska from Asia and spread to South America by 12,000. **c.6000** A form of maize is grown in Peru and Mexico. **c.6000** Llamas (right) are used as pack animals in Peru. **c.5000** Fishermen in California make large canoes.	**c.4000** North American hunters build temporary villages of grass huts. **c.3500** Pacific fishing villages in South America grow cotton for cloth. **c.3500** Pottery is made from Mexico to Peru. **c.3500** North American hunters use weighted spear throwers.	**c.3000** Most people in Central America live in settled villages. **c.2500** Maize is the chief food crop in Mexico and Central America.	**c.1800** Ancestors of the Inuit settle in Arctic Canada. **c.1800** Temple-towns are built in South America. **c.1100** The Olmec civilisation is established in southern Mexico.
EUROPE	**c.38,000** Human beings reach southern Europe. **c.20,000** Hunters paint animals on cave walls in France and Spain. **c.10,000** Shelters are made of animal bones in Russia. **c.5000** Farming spreads from the Middle East.	**c.4000** Stone graves are made in Britanny, France. **c.4000** Crop-growing begins in Britain and Ireland. **c.3500** Ploughs are used in parts of Europe. **c.3500** Farmers in Germany build wooden houses on stilts.	**c.3000** Objects are made of bronze, cast in moulds in the Mediterranean region. **c.3000** The stone village of Skara Brae is built in the Orkney Isles, Scotland. **c.2700** The building of Stonehenge (left) begins in England. **c.2200** Bronze becomes common through most of Europe.	**c.2000** The Minoan civilisation begins in Crete and lasts until c.1450. **c.1600** The Mycenaean civilisation begins in Greece and lasts until c.1200. **c.1200** Celts from central Europe move to the west.
ASIA and OCEANIA	**c.6000** Signs of farming exist in the Indus valley. **c.6000** Pigs are kept in northern China. **c.5000** Farmers in south-east Asia and China learn to grow rice. **c.5000** Hand-painted pottery is made in central China.	**c.4000** Fruit trees are grown in northern China. **c.4000** Large villages in northern China are laid out according to a plan. **c.4000** Chinese craftsmen develop new kinds of pottery.	**c.3000** Chinese farmers use ploughs. **c.3000** Chinese potters increase production with the potter's wheel. **c.3000** Metal objects are made in south-east Asia. **c.2400** Towns appear in the Indus valley. **c.2200** Farm animals in the Indus valley include zebu (hump-backed cattle).	**c.1760** The rich Shang kingdom exists in Henan, China, and lasts until c.1125. **c.1500** Polynesian settlers reach Tonga and Samoa by boat (left). **c.1500** Elaborate bronze vessels are made in Shang China. **c.1450** The Indus valley towns are destroyed by earthquakes and invasion.
AFRICA and MIDDLE EAST	**c.40,000** Human beings (*homo sapiens*) are living in Africa. **c.8000** The first city of Jericho is built. **c.7500** Houses of mud bricks are made in Mesopotamia. **c.6000** Herdsmen tame wild cattle in North Africa. **c.6000** Channels are dug to water crops, cloth is woven for clothes and clay pots are made for cooking. **c.5500** The first metal tools (copper) are made in Mesopotamia. **c.5000** People in the Nile valley (Egypt) grow grain and keep animals.	**c.4000** Dams and reservoirs are made in Iran. **c.4000** Mesopotamian farmers use simple ploughs (left). **c.4000** Sharp stone knives with bone handles are made in Egypt. **c.3500** Large temples are built in Mesopotamia. **c.3500** Sailing boats are used on the Nile. **c.3200** The Sumerians develop the earliest form of writing. **c.3100** Menes unites Upper and Lower Egypt as one kingdom.	**c.3000** The wheel is in use for transport in Mesopotamia. **c.2800** People bury their dead at Zimbabwe, south-east Africa. **c.2700** Pyramids (below) are built as tombs for Egyptian kings. **c.2600** Egypt trades with the Middle East.	**c.2000** Some iron tools and weapons are made. **c.1780** Hammurabi publishes his laws. **c.1780** The Hyskos, foreign kings, rule Egypt until c.1550. **c.1600** The Hittites capture Babylon. **c.1400** The Phoenicians develop an alphabet. **c.1100** The Hebrews leave Egypt and return to Palestine.

Thanks to modern science, we can find out surprising details about people's lives in these far-off times, even what they ate and what illnesses they had. But some things we will never know.

1000-500 BC

c.1000 Olmec sculptors make mysterious, giant-size stone heads (below).
c.850 Chavin de Huantar becomes a big religious centre in Peru.
c.700 The Olmecs leave their chief city of San Lorenzo.
c.600 The Oaxaca civilisation replaces the Olmecs.

c.800 Homer composes the *Iliad* and the *Odyssey* in Greece.
776 The first Olympic Games are held.
c.600 Greek merchants settle at Marseilles, France.
509 The Romans create their republic.
508 Democratic government begins in Athens.

c.1000 Invaders called Aryans spread across northern India.
c.1000 The people of the Jomon culture produce the first-known works of Japanese art.
557 King Cyrus unites the Medes and the Persians.

c.940 King Solomon of Israel builds the first temple in Jerusalem.
c.900 The kingdom of Kush is created in the Sudan.
c.900 Clay heads (left) are made by the people of the Nok culture in Nigeria.
814 The Phoenicians found Carthage in North Africa.
c.600 King Nebuchadnezzar builds the Hanging Gardens of Babylon (right).

500 BC–AD 1

c.500 The Zapotecs, successors of the Oaxaca, begin their ceremonial capital of Monte Albán, southern Mexico.
c.300 The Maya population in Central America begins to increase sharply due to improved farming methods.

479 The Greeks defeat a Persian invasion.
438 The Parthenon is built in Athens.
431 The Peloponnesian War begins, ending with Athens defeated in 404.
49 Julius Caesar conquers Gaul.
27 Augustus become the first Roman emperor.

c.480 Two great religious leaders die: Buddha (below) in India, Confucius in China.
322 Chandragupta founds the Mauryan empire in India.
221 The Qin dynasty unites China.
110 The Chinese open the Silk Road across central Asia.

332 Alexander the Great conquers Egypt. In 331 he conquers the whole Persian empire.
c.300 Jewish traders settle in Egypt and Syria.
c.300 The library of Alexandria, Egypt, is founded.
c.300 Bantu-speaking tribes from West Africa begin to spread east and south.
168 The temple in Jerusalem is destroyed by Syrian rulers of Israel.
146 The Romans conquer Carthage.

AD 1-500

c.100 Teotihuacán becomes the largest centre in Mexico.
c.200 The Maya begin to use a form of writing (right).
c.250 The Maya come under the rule of godlike kings and build huge stone temples.

69 The Emperor Vespasian begins building the Colosseum (below) in Rome.
79 The Roman town of Pompeii is buried by a volcano.
117 The Roman empire reaches its greatest extent.
410 Alaric and the Goths capture Rome.
476 The last Roman emperor in the West is deposed.

c.100 The Chinese learn how to make paper.
c.100 The first people settle in Hawaii.
c.150 Buddhism spreads in China.
220 The Chinese empire is divided after the end of the Han dynasty.
c.350 The Huns begin invading India.
c.480 The Gupta empire in India begins to break up.

133 Jews flee to other countries after a failed rebellion.
c.200 An Arab people in Jordan build Petra (right) in Greek style.
330 Constantinople becomes the capital of the Eastern Roman (Byzantine) empire.
396 St Augustine, Christian teacher, becomes Bishop of Hippo in Algeria.
c.400 The empire of Aksum controls most of highland Ethiopia and the Blue Nile valley.
400 The Huns invade Iran.
c.430 The Vandals settle in North Africa.

500-600

c.550 Mayan civilisation reaches its greatest development.

527 Justinian becomes Byzantine emperor and regains much of the old empire in the West.

535 The last Gupta ruler in India dies.
581 China is reunited under the Sui dynasty.
571 Prince Shokotu begins to organise the imperial government in Japan.
594 Buddhism becomes the chief religion of Japan.

c.570 Nubia, in north-east Africa, becomes Christian.
579 The Sassanid Empire of Persia reaches its greatest extent.

Who's Who

Alexander the Great (356-323 BC), king of Macedon. He led a Greek army against the Persians and in 13 years conquered an empire that stretched from Greece to India. His empire did not last long after his death, but it spread Greek ideas in Asia and brought Eastern influences into the Mediterranean world.

Archimedes (died 212 BC), Greek inventor. He invented a water pump which used the principle of the screw. Another famous discovery, made in his bath, was the 'Archimedian principle', that the weight lost by a body in water equals the weight of the water the body displaces.

Aristotle (384-322 BC), Greek philosopher. He had a school in Athens and was for a time tutor to Alexander the Great. He lectured and wrote on many subjects, from plays and poetry to politics and plant life. He is still considered one of the world's greatest thinkers, nearly 2,000 years after his death.

Augustus (63 BC-AD 14), first Roman emperor. Born Octavian, he was the nephew and heir of Julius Caesar. He became ruler of the Roman world after defeating his rival, Mark Antony, and was given the title Augustus ('Exalted') by the Senate in 27 BC. His reign was a golden period, especially for literature and architecture.

Caesar, Julius (100-44 BC), Roman ruler. He conquered Gaul (France) and invaded Britain (55 and 54 BC). The most powerful man in the empire, he marched into Italy (49 BC) against orders from the Senate. He defeated his rival, Pompey, and became dictator. He was murdered by a group of jealous noblemen.

Cleopatra (69-30 BC), queen of Egypt. She was supported by the Roman leader, Julius Caesar, and later by his chief supporter, Mark Antony. At the battle of Actium (31 BC), her ships deserted Antony, who was defeated by the forces of Octavian (Augustus). Having failed to win over Octavian, she killed herself.

Constantine (died AD 337), Roman emperor. He became sole emperor in 324 after defeating several rivals. He founded an eastern capital of the empire at Byzantium, renaming it Constantinople after himself. He made Christianity a legal religion, calling the Council of Nycaea (AD 325) to settle differences in Christian beliefs.

Cyrus the Great (died 529 BC), founder of the Persian empire. After uniting the Medes and the Persians, he conquered Babylon in 539 BC. He was more generous than most conquerors and allowed the Jews, held captive in Babylon, to return home. His dynasty, the Achaemaenids, ruled the huge Persian empire until 331 BC.

Heraclius (died AD 641), Byzantine (East Roman) emperor. The Byzantine Empire was in a state of collapse when Heraclius became emperor in 610. He built up the amy and in six years defeated all enemies, including the Persians, who had almost captured the city. In the 630s he was unable to stop new invaders, the Arabs.

Hadrian (AD 76-138), Roman emperor from 117. Travels throughout the empire convinced him that it was too large to defend. He fixed its eastern border at the River Euphrates and its northern border at Hadrian's Wall in Britain. He admired Greek civilisation, and built many fine buildings in Rome and other places.

Hannibal (247-183 BC), Carthaginian general. In 218 BC he invaded Italy by crossing the Alps from Spain with an army including elephants. He defeated the Romans in Italy, but could not capture Rome. After 15 years in Italy, he returned to defend Carthage from a Roman attack and was defeated at the battle of Zama (202 BC).

Hippocrates (died 377 BC), Greek doctor. Called the 'father of medicine', he lived on the island of Cos and his taught students to rely on facts and examination. Most of what we know of him is legend, and he may not be the author of the ancient code of good behaviour for doctors called the 'Hippocratic oath'.

Justinian (AD 483-565), Byzantine (East Roman) emperor. With his wife Theodora, he reigned over a brilliant court. He is remembered best for his collection of Roman law and his buildings, especially the Church of St. Sophia. His generals and his barbarian allies won back most of the western empire for a short time.

Pacal (AD 603-683), Mayan king of Palenque, 615-683. During the reign of Pacal and his son, Palenque controlled many other Mayan cities. Fine buildings were erected in Palenque, including a 20-metre tower. Pacal, who was only 5 feet tall, was still leading his army when he was 70.

Pericles (died 429 BC), leader of Athens. His intelligence and character made him the greatest man in Athens, and the brilliant artists he employed made the city more beautiful. He foresaw the coming war with Sparta (431 BC) and made plans for it that were at first successful, though he died of plague before it began.

Ptolemy (2nd century AD), Greek scholar of Alexandria. The study of astronomy and geography in Europe was based on his writings until the 16th century. He believed that the Earth is the centre of the universe, and thought it smaller than it really is. This influenced Columbus's voyage to America in 1492.

Rameses II (?1290-1224 BC), king of Egypt. One of the greatest warrior pharaohs, he is remembered for his war against the Hittites in Syria, and for his massive buildings. They included the Temple of Amun at Karnak, the largest religious building in the world, and the Temple of Abu Simbel, with giant statues of himself.

Taharqa (reigned 690-664 BC), king of Egypt. He belonged to the 25th Dynasty, Kushites from Nubia in the south. Taharqa reigned during a period of prosperity, and he built many temples and monuments. Growing rivalry with Assyria led to defeat soon after his death, and the Kushite kings gave up Egypt.

Glossary

absolute ruler A king or other ruler whose power is not limited by laws.

acropolis The ceremonial centre in ancient Greek cities, where the chief temples were built. It usually stood on high ground.

aqueduct A bridge which carries water in a canal or channel over a valley.

archaeology The study of the past, especially the prehistoric past, through the evidence of actual remains.

Asia Minor The region of Asia nearest to Europe, roughly the same as modern Turkey.

barbarian The name used by the ancient Greeks to describe all peoples who were not Greek, and by Romans for non-Romans. The word came to mean wild and uncivilised.

basilica A large, rectangular, public building in ancient Rome. Early Christian churches usually took this form, with a central aisle, or walkway.

Bronze Age The ancient time when people had learned to make metal tools and weapons, especially of bronze, but had not yet learned to make iron. This happened at different times in different places.

calendar A system for dividing up the year into seasons, months and days, usually by the movements of the Sun and stars.

calligraphy Beautiful handwriting. It was one of the chief forms of art in ancient Egypt, in the monasteries of Europe, and in China and Japan.

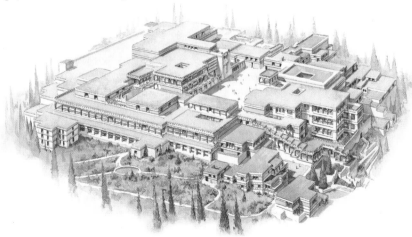

chariot A fast, two-wheeled, horse-drawn cart used in ancient warfare.

city-state A state made up of one city with surrounding country and villages.

civilisation A group of people who have reached a state of development that includes living in cities, organised government, a written language, fine arts and learning.

cuneiform Meaning 'wedge-shaped', the early form of writing in Mesopotamia.

democracy A country or form of government where power depends on the votes of the people.

dictator A ruler with supreme power, above the law. In Ancient Rome, dictators were elected in a time of crisis.

dissenters People who disagree with accepted laws or beliefs, especially in religion.

empire A state which also controls other people or states.

economy The management of the whole wealth of a state (or another type of community), including money, trade, and industry.

Fertile Crescent A region in the Middle East, which was one of the earliest centres of farming. It stretched from the Nile valley, north-east along the eastern Mediterranean and south-east through the valleys of the Tigris and Euphrates rivers.

finance The management of all money matters.

galley A type of ship driven mainly by oars, though some also had sails.

gladiator In ancient Rome, a man who fought in an arena to entertain an audience. Gladiators were often prisoners or slaves.

hegira The journey of the Prophet Muhammad from Mecca to Medina in AD 622, the first year of the Muslim calendar.

hereditary title A title that is passed down in one family, from its holder to his or her heir.

heresy A religious belief that opposes the accepted beliefs of the time.

hominid A creature like a human being, an ancestor of the human race.

Ice Age A period when the Earth's climate was much colder, with much of the northern continents covered by ice. The last Ice Age ended about 10,000 BC.

Glossary

icon A religious picture or sculpture, especially a picture of a saint in the Orthodox Christian Church.

Iron Age The period when humans had learned to use iron, following the Bronze Age.

irrigation Watering of fields by the use of canals or channels.

legend A story that is probably based on true events.

loom A machine on which yarn, or thread, is woven into cloth.

mandarin A government official in the Chinese Empire.

mercenary A professional soldier, willing to fight for anyone who pays him.

Middle East The region of south-west Asia from the Mediterranean to Afghanistan.

mosaic A picture made up of many small stone or glass cubes of different colours.

mosque A Muslim place of worship.

mutiny A rebellion by soldiers or sailors.

neanderthal An early type of human being in Europe, another type of homo sapiens, or modern man.

Near East The region around the eastern Mediterranean, sometimes including Egypt and south-east Europe.

papyrus A kind of paper made from reeds, cut into strips and pressed into sheets. It was used by the ancient Egyptians, Greeks and Romans.

patricians The nobles, members of the Senate, in ancient Rome.

patriotism A person's love of his or her country.

peasant The lowest class of country people, usually farm workers. Some peasants owned their own land.

philosophy The study of the basic truths on which human life and thinking are based.

plebeians The ordinary citizens of ancient Rome.

pottery Vases, cups, plates and other vessels made from clay and baked hard.

prehistoric Belonging to a time 'before history', which means before written records were kept.

prophet Someone who was believed to speak God's message.

pueblo A village community living in a large building built of adobe (clay) or stone in what is now the south-western USA.

pyramid A huge, square, stone building whose four sides slope up to a point. In ancient Egypt, they contained the tombs of kings.

senate The assembly of patricians in ancient Rome. In many countries today, the senate is one of the two assemblies that make up the legislature.

shrine A holy place or building, such as the tomb of a saint, which pilgrims visit.

siege An attack on a castle or town defended by stone walls.

statesman A politician or government official of great ability, especially one who has an influence on international affairs.

Stone Age The time before human beings learned to use metals, and made tools from stone.

stupa A Buddhist monument, usually in the shape of a dome, which marks a holy place.

tyrant A ruler who holds supreme power, above the law. It has become a name for an evil dictator who holds power by force.

ziggurat A religious building like a pyramid, but with sides that rise in a series of steps.

Index

Index

Index

Acknowledgements

Picture research by Caroline Wood

The publisher would like to thank the following for illustrations:

Richard Berridge; p8t
Chris Brown; p10c, p110b, p19l, p28, p37b, p39tr
Tim Clarey; 29br, p42
Mike Codd; p9tr
Peter Connolly; p22tr, p22-23b, p24b, p26, p28t, p30-31b
Gino D'Achille; back cover, p66-67
Gino D'Achille and Robbie Polley; p40-41
Richard Hook; p14-15b, p38-39b
Barbara Lofthouse; p50b
Steve Noon; Back cover bl, p12-13b, p20b, p21b
Olive Pearson; all maps
Martin Sanders; p33t

The publisher would like to thank the following for permission to use photographs:

Front cover BAL "Louvre, Paris, France, Giraudon"; p9c BM; p11b ET; p12t BM; p13t BM; p13bc BM; p15tl Boltin Picture Library; p15c MH, BM; p16-17b Bildarchiv Preussischer Kulturbesitz, Klaus Goken; p17ct MH, BM; p17b BM; p18bl Telegraph Colour Library, Mauro Carraro; p19r AKG, "Delhi National Museum,Jean-Louis Nou"; p20-21 c AKG, Heraklion Archaeological Museum; p21tr MH, BM; p23tr MH, BM; p24t MH, BM; p25t ET; p25c AKG, "Musée du Louvre, Paris. Erich Lessing"; p27bc AKG, "The Archaeological Museum, Istanbul, Erich Lessing"; p27cr AKG, "Liebighaus, Frankfurt, Erich Lessing"; p29t AKG; p30t ET, "Staatliche Glypothek, Munich"; p31t Magnum, Dennis Stock; p32l ET; p33br MH, BM; p34b AKG, "Byzantine Museum, Athens, Erich Lessing"; p34r ET; p35t AKG; p36t MH, "Musée Guimet,Paris"; p36b AKG, Jean-Louis Nou; p37t AKG, Erich Lessing; p38t AKG, "National Archaeological Museum,Guatemala, Erich Lessing"; p38bl ET, Museum of Mankind

Key: BAL = Bridgeman Art Library; BM = The British Museum; ET = E.T. Archive; AKG = AKG London; MH = Michael Holford